CARLISLE CATHEDRAL

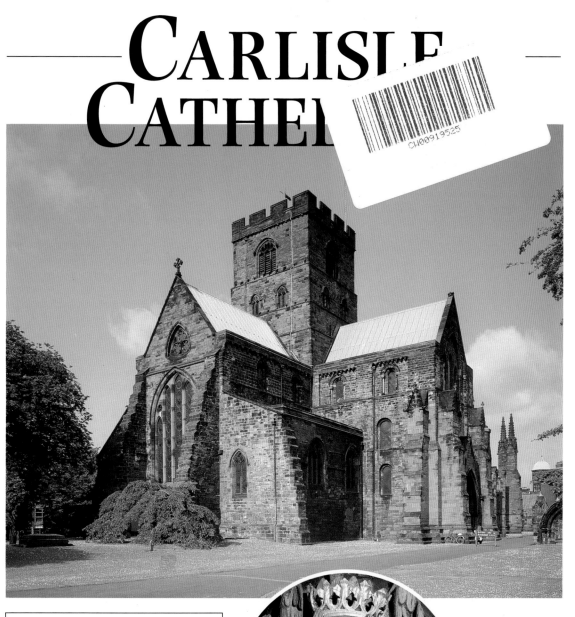

Contents

Above:
The cathedral, showing the Norman south transept and the remaining two bays of the nave.

Left: ②
A boss depicting the Coronation of Our Lady, situated under the organ screen. The priory was dedicated to the Blessed Virgin Mary. In 1541 the title was altered to the Cathedral Church of the Holy and Undivided Trinity.

Dean's Welcome

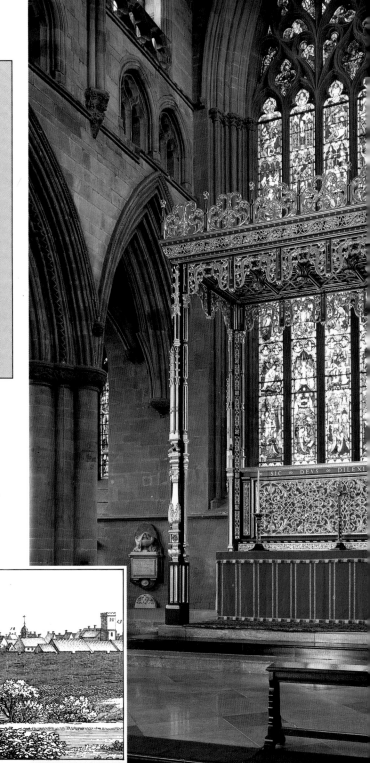

Carlisle Cathedral has a special atmosphere, of prayer and worship. This comes partly from the fact that Christians have worshipped God in this building for nearly 900 years – and on this site for hundreds of years before – partly because this is a building complete in the beauty of holiness. Some stones from the Roman city or Hadrian's Wall are now built into the fabric. The beauty of the Fells and the Lakes is reflected in the beauty of this place. We hope you enjoy your visit to the place we call the House of God, the Gate of Heaven. We pray you will also become aware of God's presence here. God be with you and bless you on your way.

Below:
The skyline in 1745 with the west walls in the foreground, from an engraving by Buck. Prior Slee's Gateway is on the left (7), the Deanery in the centre (10) and St Cuthbert's Church on the right (13). The modern view opposite shows that the cathedral is largely unchanged.

Right: ⑨
The high altar baldachino designed by Sir Charles Nicholson in 1934, and gilded by Stephen Dykes Bower; the silver cross and candlesticks were given in memory of Henry Williams (Bishop 1920–46). The medieval high altar stood one bay further west.

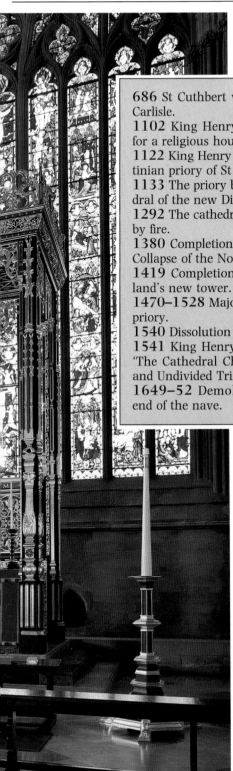

686 St Cuthbert visits Christians in Carlisle.

1102 King Henry I grants the site for a religious house.

1122 King Henry founds the Augustinian priory of St Mary.

1133 The priory becomes the cathedral of the new Diocese of Carlisle.

1292 The cathedral partly destroyed by fire.

1380 Completion of the new choir. Collapse of the Norman bell tower.

1419 Completion of Bishop Strickland's new tower.

1470–1528 Major rebuilding of the priory.

1540 Dissolution of the priory.

1541 King Henry VIII incorporates 'The Cathedral Church of the Holy and Undivided Trinity'.

1649–52 Demolition of the west end of the nave.

1660 The parish church returns to the east end of the nave.

1745 Jacobite rebels imprisoned in the remains of the nave.

1764–68 Internal restoration under Bishop Lyttleton.

1853–56 Restoration under Dean Tait.

1870 Parish church removed to new site in grounds.

1934 Dean Cooper founds the Friends of the Cathedral.

1958 Restoration under Dean Mayne.

1978 Queen Elizabeth II distributes the Royal Maundy.

1989 Excavations uncover the site of the early burial ground.

1990 Opening of the treasury.

1991 Queen Elizabeth II visits on the 450th anniversary of the foundation of the Dean and Chapter.

3

The Early Church

An earlier church close to the present cathedral had long been suspected by the number of 8th to 10th-century cross fragments found in the vicinity. Evidence of the Christian graveyard, used between 700 and 1000 came with excavations in 1985 and 1989. Viking-age objects were found, and the burials may have been those of immigrants, perhaps even real Vikings! It is probable that the existing church was removed to make way for the priory church, and its site could be somewhere beneath the demolished cloister. As the priory church took the place of the parish church it was necessary to make provision within the new church for the parishioners. The dual role as parish church and cathedral continued until 1870.

The division of the city into two parishes possibly pre-dated the construction of the priory. The unusual fact that nearby St Cuthbert's Church is

Right:
A fragment of an 8th-century cross found in extending No. 3, The Abbey. Translation of the inscription: Sig ( ) set this up in memory of (SU) itberht.

orientated north to south rather than east to west suggests that it stands on a Roman street and is probably of pre-Conquest date. St Cuthbert visited Carlisle in 686, viewing the remains of the Roman town then still standing and a monastery which has not yet been located. King Ecgfrith gave to the saint a considerable area around, known as the 'Patrimony of St Cuthbert'. This meant that St Cuthbert's community and their successors at Durham Cathedral had jurisdiction here till the foundation of the Diocese of Carlisle in 1133.

Another place of Christian worship was St Alban's Chapel in Scotch Street whose dedication indicates an early date.

Above: ⑦
This figure on a stall canopy illustrates an Augustinian canon. He wears the distinctive robes including a biretta (hat). In 1258 Pope Alexander IV gave the canons at Carlisle special permission to wear these in church because of the cold here.

Left:
The excavation in preparation for the treasury. This went down to Anglo-Saxon and Roman levels.

Right: ⑥
This painting in the north aisle from the Life of St Cuthbert depicts how 'He was guided by an eagle flying aloft And fed by a dolphin as ye see.'

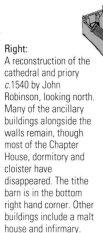

Right:
A reconstruction of the cathedral and priory c.1540 by John Robinson, looking north. Many of the ancillary buildings alongside the walls remain, though most of the Chapter House, dormitory and cloister have disappeared. The tithe barn is in the bottom right hand corner. Other buildings include a malt house and infirmary.

Below:
An engraving by Kyp showing the demolished west end of the nave. Beyond at the left is the fratry, to the right the Prior's tower and Deanery. Its windows have hardly changed.

Whatever buildings were on this site, the first priest named is Walter who was responsible for the care of St Mary's parishioners. In 1122 King Henry I replaced the original building by founding the priory. Ten years later, perhaps more to consolidate the Border than for any ecclesiastical motive, he created the Diocese of Carlisle. So the priory church became the cathedral, Adelulf of Nostell in Yorkshire its first Bishop. Most medieval cathedrals were ruled by Benedictine monks; Carlisle was unique in being in the care of Augustinian canons.

Part of Adelulf's church survives, of Norman design and cruciform in plan. The arms of the cross followed the same lines as the present crossing with two smaller apses flanking a large one which contained the sanctuary and extended into the choir. The church's change in status required the enlargement of the latter: the need for side altars to celebrate mass for the dead increased the number of side chapels. Only one survives, St Catherine's by the south door. In 1292 a fire, deliberately started in the suburbs by a disinherited son, spread throughout the city and caused considerable damage which necessitated further rebuilding.

In the 14th century the upper walls of the choir were rebuilt. At the beginning of the 15th century, in Bishop Strickland's time, a new tower was completed to replace the Norman one that fell on the north transept. Maintenance of the fabric has continued every century since, with an extensive alteration to the ceiling in the 18th, and Ewan Christian's thoroughgoing restoration in the 19th. Continuous conservation is in progress today.

The Nave

The nave and transepts formed part of the church begun in 1122. Architectural details resemble Melbourne in Derbyshire where the Bishop of Carlisle had a manor. The 12th-century work is contemporary with the earliest stonework in Carlisle Castle, probably from the same quarries and by the same craftsmen. The existing two and a half bays show that building was in two stages: the way the pilasters in the aisles stop at ceiling level demonstrates the change in design.

Distortion of several aisle arches may reflect subsidence of Roman deposits beneath a drying out of the foundations in a series of parched summers. The western part consisted of seven bays and five of these formed the Parish Church of St Mary. Demolition of five bays of the nave in the Commonwealth period reduced St Mary's to the two bays that remained. Stones from the west end were used in repairing the cathedral. In 1745 and 1746 Jacobites were imprisoned briefly in the parish church.

Sir Walter Scott the novelist was married here in 1797. In the 19th century, the population increased and services in St Mary's interfered with services in the choir. Hence a new church was built in 1870 by Ewan Christian.

Regimental standards have hung in the nave for many years, but in 1949 this became the Border Regiment Chapel. The Gideon and west windows (1870) are by Hardman. Bishop Waldegrave's effigy (1872) is by John Adams Acton. In the north aisle is the Virgin and Child, *I am the Life* (1990) by Josephina de Vasconcellos; a window (1985) by Harry Harvey, *The Baptism of Christ*; a tapestry *The County of Cumbria* (1989) and the font (1891) by Sir Arthur Blomfield.

There are eight bells, the oldest dating from 1401. The peal was increased from four to six 1657–59. Two more were added when the bells were restored in memory of Dean Rashdall in 1926.

The north transept, St Wilfrid's Chapel, contains the Brougham triptych. The main window commemorates five daughters of Dean Tait who in 1856 died of scarlet fever within six weeks of each other. Each scene contains an arum lily, a reminder that one daughter could not accurately repeat the 23rd Psalm, but said 'Though I walk through the lily of the valley of death'. Above is stained glass (1857) by John Scott of Carlisle; the west window (1846) by Wailes; a memorial to John Johnston (1800) by an associate of Nollekens; a medieval alabaster Crucifixion; a statue of St Barbara and the tomb of Prior Senhouse (d.1520).

The south transept was pierced by Ewan Christian for the main entrance. Above is a window, *The Seven Days of Creation* (1883) by Clayton and Bell, and in the shop one by Christopher Whall (1916). St Catherine's Chapel has in its tracery the initials of Prior Gondibour (c.1465–94).

Above:
Excerpt from the marriage registry of St Mary's Church, recording the novelist Sir Walter Scott's marriage in 1797. He married from Castle Street, and a plaque marks the house.

Opposite: ③
The King's Own Royal Border Regiment chapel, created in 1949 to the design of Stephen Dykes Bower in the remains of the nave. The flat wall shows where the choir stalls were in the time of the Norman priory.

Below:
The east end of the nave when it was used as the Parish Church of St Mary, complete with box pews. The font was replaced with one by Blomfield in 1891.

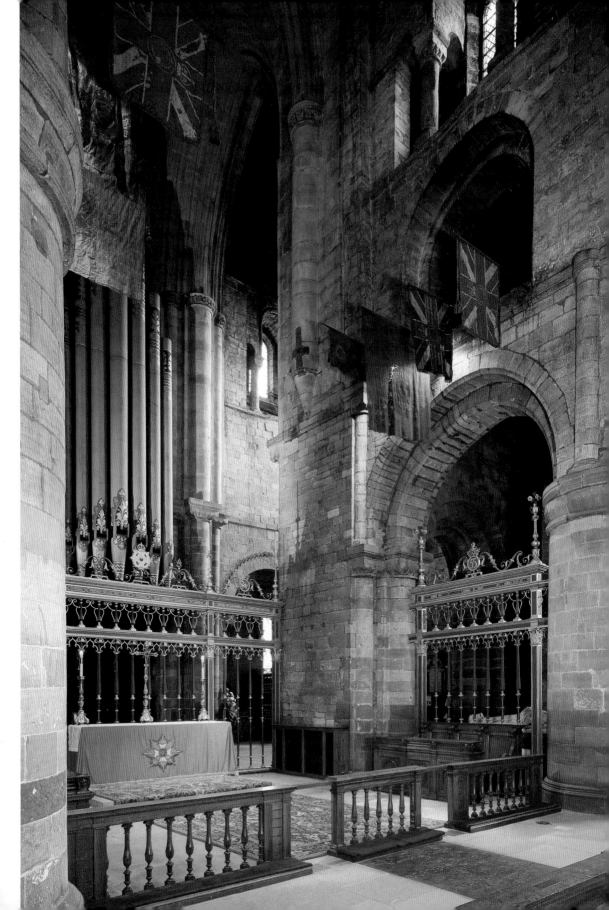

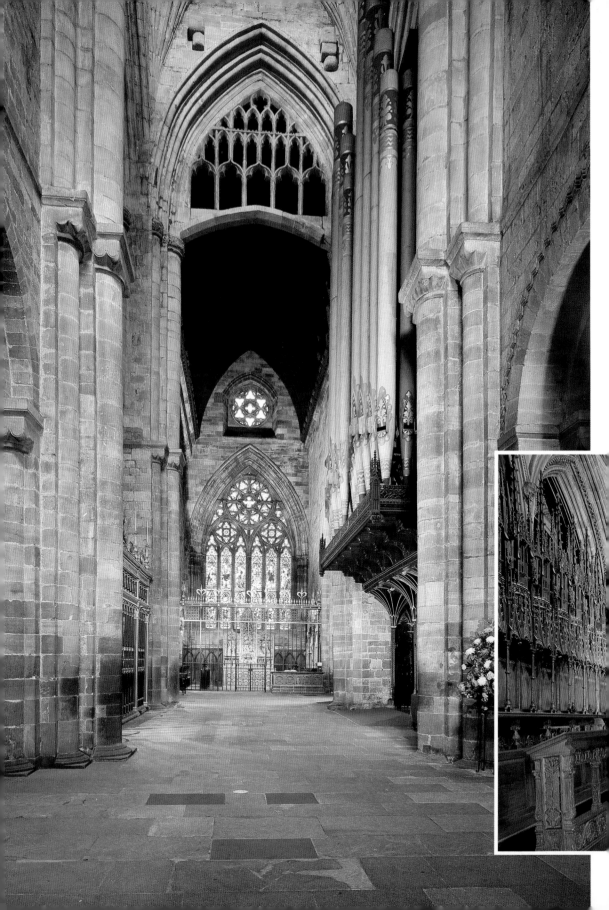

The Choir

Opposite: ①
The view from the south door to the St Wilfred's Chapel in the north transept. Prior Senhouse's tomb is in front of the screen. The stained glass window designed by Hardman commemorates Dean Tait's children.

Below: ⑦
The 15th-century choir stalls. The pinnacles were added later. The choir benches by Nicholson were extended by Stephen Dykes Bower in 1975. The first Bishop was the Prior so he retained his seat on the south side; in other cathedrals he would sit on the north.

From the beginning, canons have assembled beneath the 13th-century walls of the choir to offer their worship – and so they do today. The 1292 fire necessitated the replacement of the piers, which now support earlier arcades.

Its glory is the 15th-century stalls. The elaborate tops to the canopies (tabernacle work) date from c.1455. They were originally gilded and painted with figures in the niches. Below each stall is a misericord carved with subjects taken from legend or from books of beasts (bestiaries). Under that marked 'Cancellarius' is a mermaid. The stalls are for the 24 honorary canons, office holders in the cathedral, city and county: the Bishop's is on the south side, the Dean's on the north. The titles above are in Latin.

Left:
Underneath each seat in the choir stalls is a carved misericord, to support the occupants while standing. The canons of the cathedral have their stalls here and also office holders in the city and county.

The doors on the 'return' stalls (1765) are by Thomas Pitt. The graffiti were probably carved by grammar school boys who had their lessons here. The choir-stalls date from 1910, being doubled in length in 1975 in memory of Dr Wadely, Organist 1910–60. In the floor is the fine brass of Bishop Bell (d.1496), formerly Prior of Durham.

The organ (1856) is by Henry (Father) Willis, rebuilt in 1907 by Harrison and Harrison, and in 1962 by J.W. Walker. A predecessor mentioned in 1571 was given to Appleby church in 1684, and another of 1808 sold to Hexham Abbey in 1856. Over the last 150 years most organists have given long service. Henry Ford (1842–1902) came to Carlisle by stagecoach. Sydney Nicholson (later Sir Sydney, 1902–08) was founder of the Royal School of Church Music. Wadely, mentioned above, served for half a century and his successor, Andrew Seivewright for 31 years to 1991.

The stunning view from the organ loft of the 15th-century stalls and 14th-century east window. The painted ceiling was restored to its medieval shape by Owen Jones in 1856, and repainted in 1970. The bosses reproduce the shields of benefactors.

The Presbytery

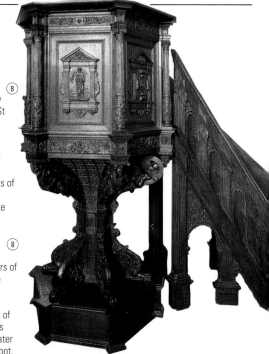

This is the area from the choir to the east wall, dominated by the 14th-century east window. York Minster, Selby Abbey and several churches in Lincolnshire have similar tracery, which may all be the work of one Ivo de Raughton from Raughton Head. The top of the window is medieval, depicting the last judgement. Christ guides the blessed to paradise; the wicked are cast into the red fires of hell. The lower panels contain scenes from the life of Christ (1861) by Hardman. Both glass and stonework were restored in 1982.

The high altar has a baldachino (1936) designed by Sir Charles Nicholson, gilded by Stephen Dykes Bower in 1970. Here the central act of worship the Holy Eucharist is offered every Sunday.

Around the presbytery and choir, the 14th-century capitals depict the Labours of the Month, a series illustrating the activities of the medieval farmer. January shows a man with two faces, like the god Janus. In February another sits over a fire and pours water from his boot. March has him pruning vines; directly opposite is September when he gathers grapes. Above is the magnificent ceiling (1856) by Owen Jones, who decorated the Great Exhibition of 1851. When the Dean first saw it, he exclaimed 'Oh my stars!'

Looking down over the presbytery steps is the face of the Blessed Virgin Mary. Carlisle was once an important centre of devotion to her. The Bishop's throne (1874) is by G. E. Street. Immediately to the west is a corbel said to depict Dean Close's dog, Tyree. The lectern (1944) is by Stephen Dykes Bower. On the north is the 16th-century Salkeld screen and beside, the pulpit purchased in 1970 in memory of Dean Mayne (1943–59).

The backs of the stalls are painted with, as it were, medieval strip cartoons.

Right: ⑧
The pulpit, originally from the Church of St Andrews, Antwerp, dated 1559; brought here from Cockayne Hatley in memory of Dean Mayne. Four frames depict figures of the evangelists, Matthew, Mark, Luke and John; the fifth, ornamental roses.

Below: ⑧
The stone capitals represent the Labours of the Month. This one shows the month of February where the peasant sits in front of the fire, warming his toes and pouring water from his upturned boot.

Right:
The Salkeld screen, Renaissance woodwork presented by the last Prior who became the first Dean, probably in gratitude for the royal favour. The coat of arms is of King Henry VIII. The letters G(od) S(ave) P(rince) E(dward) and the feathers denote his son. Also inscribed is L(ancelot) S(alkeld) D(ecanus) K(arliolensis).

In the south aisle is the story of St Augustine, in the north that of St Antony who converted him, and of St Cuthbert who had strong local links through his friendship with St Herbert of Derwentwater. A fourth depicts the Twelve Apostles, each with the clause of the creed he had contributed.

At the east end of the north aisle is an altar on whose riddel posts are the figures of St Cuthbert, King Ecgfrith, King Henry I and Prior Adelulf. The window above (1893) is by Clayton and Bell. Towards the west is the grave of Archdeacon Paley (d.1805) whose *Evidences for Christianity* was long an exam-

Below left: ⑦
The Bishop's throne or
cathedra (from which
the word cathedral
comes). It was designed
by G. E. Street in 1880.
The arms of Bishop
Harvey Goodwin are
above.

Right: ⑨
The east window. The
tracery was begun in the
14th century but not
completed until the
19th. The upper lights
show the Last
Judgement with Christ
in Glory and were
restored by York Glaziers
Trust; the lower, scenes
from the Life of Christ by
Hardman (1861).

ination text at Oxford and Cambridge.
On the doors of the cope chest is painted
the broom bush, the crest of the Plan-
tagenets, which dates it to the 14th century. Amongst the names carved is
Sawrey Gilpin (1747), later to become a
famous painter and Royal Academecian.
The chamber organ (1990) is by
Walker's. A stained glass window commemorates Henry Edmund Ford
(d.1902); the Mothers' Union banner is
in memory of Alice Bennett and a tablet
to the Revd Theodore Hardy VC, DSO,
MC (d.1918), a World War I padre.

The east window of the south aisle
by Wailes commemorates John Heysham
(1753–1834), a local doctor who by
studying deaths formulated the *Carlisle
Tables of Mortality*, used by insurers as a
basis for life expectancy. In the south
wall arcade is a head, thought to be that

Below: ⑪
St Catherine's Chapel
screen. The cathedral
had a considerable
quantity of decorative
woodwork, much of
which was removed in
the 19th century. Note
the initials T G for
Thomas Gondibour, Prior
here c.1465–94.

of King Edward I. Here in 1297 he received the allegiance of Robert the Bruce, sworn upon the sword that slew Thomas à Becket. From here he went to face the Scots and died at nearby Sandsfield Marsh. Adjacent are the memorials to Sir James Graham Bt., Home Secretary 1841–47; John Bardsley, Bishop 1892–1904 (by Andreo Carlo Luchesi, 1906); to Hastings Rashdall,

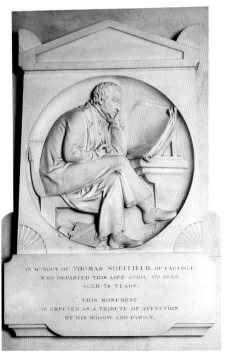

IN MEMORY OF THOMAS SHEFFIELD, OF CARLISLE,
WHO DEPARTED THIS LIFE APRIL 4TH 1853,
AGED 78 YEARS.

THIS MONUMENT
IS ERECTED AS A TRIBUTE OF AFFECTION
BY HIS WIDOW AND FAMILY.

Right: ⑱
Bishop Smith's library.
Thomas Smith was Dean in
1671 and later Bishop of
Carlisle 1684–1702. He was
a considerable benefactor of
the cathedral, presenting
communion plate and his
extensive library which is
now in the fratry. A plan to
reconstruct the dormitory as
a library in 1693 came to
nothing and this tiny building
was built instead.

Dean 1917–24 (the inscription from Origen reads 'It is better to have faith and to succeed than to have faith alone.'); to Canon Frederick Rawnsley, 1851–1928, a founder of the National Trust, poet and lover of the Lake District; to Dean Francis Close (by H. H. Armstead, who designed the figures on the Albert Memorial, 1885); to Bishop Harvey Goodwin (by Haymo Thornycroft, 1891); to Bishop Barrow, 1429–39 (situated against St Catherine's Chapel).

Right: ④
A medieval jet crucifix found during the excavations to prepare for the treasury.

Left: ①
A 19th-century memorial to Thomas Sheffield, a Carlisle dentist. Surprisingly, the tools around him are those of an engineer. The cathedral has a remarkable collection of portraits on memorials.

The large quantity of parish church plate having to be hidden away caused the Chapter in 1987 to consider creating a treasury. It would have been difficult to obtain permission for a new building above ground, so it was decided to build one below the demolished nave. Roman foundations were exposed and from the excavations came a fine jet crucifix and a tiny figure of the Virgin and Child.

Panels in the treasury describe the growth of Christianity in Cumbria. On display is church plate from the cathedral and the diocese, the Williamson collection of cathedral goblets, the verge (or wand) used by Bishop Oglethorpe at the coronation of Elizabeth I, a fine blue medieval cope of 1440 with embroidered orphreys (panels), in use until the 1980s.

The library contains collections of books given by many deans and canons, including the libraries of Bishop Thomas Smith and Isaac Milner, Dean 1791–1820, an eminent mathematician and friend of William Wilberforce. Amongst the manuscripts now lodged at the Record Office in Carlisle Castle are *Lives of the Saints* (French, 13th-century); *Romance of the Rose* (14th-century); the 16th-century Foundation Statutes; and the Machell papers about Westmorland, collected by a 17th-century incumbent of Kirkby Thore. This theological library also specializes in local history, books on the Carlisle diocese and cathedral people.

Right: ④
The treasury, excavated beneath the north aisle of the old nave and opened by the Duke of Gloucester in 1990. It contains a fine collection of cathedral and parish church silver. Here too can be seen the foundations of a great Norman nave pillar.

The Abbey

This would appear to be a misnomer, for the priory never had an abbot. But as with Durham and Bath, the Abbey has from the beginning been the name of the $4^1/_2$-acre cathedral precinct. The principal entrance is through Prior Slee's gateway at the west. (The Lorimer gates at the east end were designed by John F. Matthew and presented in 1930.) To the right of the gateway is Bishop Smith's library of 1699. Next is the Deanery. At its centre is the Prior's tower with a fine painted heraldic ceiling dating from the 16th century. It was here that Dean Close became exasperated with the noise of the engine sheds below West Walls. He sought an injunction against the railway company, but its only effect was to cause every engine that passed by to sound its whistle! To the west is the hall range modified in the 1690s to include

Above: (16)
The fratry (refectory). In the 17th century the western end became the Chapter House. Its front door and windows, blocked with new stonework in 1880, can still be seen.

Left: (17)
The Deanery, at its centre the 15th-century Prior's tower; the upper windows are 18th-century. The wing at the right dates from 1854; the lower storey extension and front door were added in 1950. Inset is a section from the 45-panel, painted ceiling of the solar, or day-room, of the tower. This was commissioned by Prior Senhouse (*c.*1494–1520) and carries his device.

a kitchen below and a solar above. In 1854 the projecting extensions were added. The south range was the domestics' quarters and beyond is a stable with Thomas Gondibour's initials above.

The fratry (formerly the refectory) became the Chapter House in the 17th century and the outlines of the door and windows are still to be seen. Street's restoration in 1881 included the reconstructed part of the Cloister Walk as a porch. Recent adornments include three tapestries (1987) by Meg Falconer and three statuettes (1990) by Josephina de Vasconcellos, *Suffer the little children to come unto Me*.

Above: (13)
This engraving shows the cloister area before G. E. Street reconstructed a fragment as the entrance to the fratry.

Above right: (14)
The cloister was the centre of the priory's domestic life. This is the doorway to the Chapter House.

Left: (19)
An engraving of Prior Slee's gateway (1840) by William Billings. This gateway was the entrance from Abbey Street. The wooden gates have never been replaced and are still in use today.

Below:
The north side of the cathedral by moonlight (1895) painted by Thomas Bushby. St Mary's Churchyard railing and gravestones were removed and the wall lowered in 1930.

To the left of the gateway is No. 2 The Abbey, dating from the 17th century. East of the fratry, No. 1 is 18th-century with later alterations. Opposite, Nos. 3 and 6, formerly one house, are late 17th-century. No. 4 (1863) is by Ewan Christian. Opposite the south entrance are the ruins of the dormitory, pierced with archways to the cloister and Chapter House.

In the 1930s, headstones were removed from the churchyard of St Mary, north of the cathedral. Part of the perimeter wall of the Abbey survives at the west extremity. The Abbey grounds are well furnished with trees, one of which is a tulip tree planted by Queen Elizabeth II in 1991.

The Cathedral Today

The cathedral as a building we have already described.

What is its purpose?

T. S. Eliot wrote 'The use of a Cathedral is the performance of the complete liturgy of the church for the Christian Year'. Hence there is the regular round of daily services, Morning and Evening Prayer, the daily Eucharist. On Sundays there is the climax of the week's worship in the Sung Eucharist. Every day on high days and holy days, saints' days and festivals, at Easter and Christmas, the liturgy is celebrated to the highest standard of music and ceremonial in the cathedral's constant pursuit of excellence. To enable this to happen there is what is called the Foundation, including not only clergy but vergers, choristers and lay clerks, whose dedication ensures the worthiness of the worship. There is no choir school. The cathedral choristers come from several schools in the city.

Secondly, the cathedral is where the Bishop has his *cathedra*, or throne, the symbol of his authority to preach and teach. This is the mother church of the diocese where diocesan services take place. Whenever there is a great occasion, an ordination, an anniversary, a commemoration, the enthronement or departure of a bishop, here people come to offer their worship. Here each of the honorary canons has his stall. From here go out the cathedral clergy to serve the diocese, one as Archdeacon, another as the Director of Education.

Thirdly, this is a place of prayer for all. The cathedral's mission extends beyond the diocese to Christians of other churches. People come to worship here who would not normally enter the door of their parish church; for example, they come in their thousands at Christmas time for Carol Services. We also have strong links with the city, the county and the King's Own Royal Border Regiment.

Right: ④
A statuette of the Blessed Virgin and Child by Josephina de Vasconcellos (1990) in the nave. A further three statuettes by the same sculptress are to be found in the fratry.

Below:
A wedding service in the cathedral.

Below: ⑯
The buttery is the former undercroft of the fratry. Many visitors come here each day for refreshments, the provision of which has always been part of the role of a monastic house.

Below right:
The cathedral has its
own workforce of skilled
craftsmen. The carving
and replacement of
stone goes on year in,
year out.

Here a regular congregation of worshippers contributes to the witness of the cathedral by their presence and their support. A large number of them assist in the Ministry of Welcome. For while the cathedral ministers to many groups of people it is above all through individuals that it extends its mission to people one by one. Nearly 200,000 visitors come here each year, to be received and welcomed by vergers, shop helpers, guides – the human face of the cathedral. People come and pray, and perhaps articulate their prayer in the lighting of a candle. They are drawn here as it were by a magnet.

Below:
The cathedral in winter.
A view from the south
east showing the 14th-
century Decorated east
window by Ivo de
Raughton, 26 feet (8m)
wide and 58 feet (18m)
high. It was fully
restored in 1982, the
sandstone for the
tracery coming from the
same Dalston quarry
that provided the
original stone in the
12th century.

Carlisle Cathedral is not perhaps the grandest of cathedrals. Biased we may be, but we reckon it is one of the most beautiful. Small we may be but 'because we are smaller, we try harder'. We are conscious of our heritage, of our privilege of serving a building of which it can truly be said, 'Surely the Lord is in this place'.

Below: ⑤
The Brougham triptych, carved in Antwerp *c.*1510. This superb altarpiece displays left: Christ on the road to Calvary, centre: the crucifixion, right: the taking down from the Cross. The scenes of the Lord's infancy below show the Circumcision, the Presentation, the Worship of the Wise Men and (misplaced) Jesse. The triptych was acquired from the continent by the Lord Chancellor, Lord Brougham, and is on loan from the parish of Brougham. It is one of only five such triptychs in Britain.